Alphabet of Rhymes

By Linda Jones
Illustrated by the Geri Livingston Studio

Based on characters originated by Lyn Wendon

Published 2004 by Collins Educational
An imprint of HarperCollins*Publishers* Ltd
77-85 Fulham Palace Road, London W6 8JB

Browse the complete Collins catalogue at
www.collinseducation.com

For non-UK supplies, please refer to:
Letterland International Ltd
Barton, Cambridge, CB3 7AY, UK

www.letterland.com

© Lyn Wendon 2004
2 4 6 8 10 9 7 5 3 1
ISBN 000 718437 9 (hardback)
ISBN 000 717952 9 (paperback)

First published 1994. This new edition published 2004.
LETTERLAND® is a registered trademark of Lyn Wendon.

British Library Cataloguing in Publication Data
A catalogue record for this publication is available from the British Library

Designed by Susi Martin
Printed by Imago

You might also like to visit
www.fireandwater.co.uk
The book lover's website

Contents

Annie Apple

Bouncy Ben

Clever Cat

Dippy Duck

Eddy Elephant

Zig Zag Zebra

**Yellow
Yo-yo Man**

Fix-it Max

About this Book

The *Letterland Alphabet of Rhymes* is a delightful collection of poems featuring the much-loved Letterland characters. Twenty-six original rhymes will take children on a magical tour of Letterland while teaching them valuable literacy concepts such as rhyme, rhythm and alliteration (a series of words starting with the same sound).

There are many ways to share this book with children to help them on the road to reading. Here are just a few ideas:

● First of all, just read the poems together. Have fun with the rhythm and rhyme. Help to look for things that start with the same letter in the beautiful illustrations, for example, the bee, butterfly, buttercup and bat on the *Bouncy Ben Plays Ball* page. Recognising initial letter sounds is one of the first steps towards successful reading.

● Re-read a poem; this time, stop before a rhyming word and say "Your turn to finish the rhyme." Call it 'our rhyming game'. Your pleasure at

Walter Walrus

Vicky Violet

Uppy Umbrella

**Talking
Tess**

Sammy Snake

Firefighter Fred

Golden Girl

Harry Hat Man

Impy Ink

Jumping Jim

Kicking King

the right responses will make it a popular game to repeat. Rhymes help children recognise the final sounds in words — a vital reading skill.

● Take turns pointing out the Letterlanders' names in the titles and poems. This will encourage important whole word recognition skills. Come back to favourite poems often, and you'll soon find other words become easily recognisable as well.

● Talk about the characters together. For example, which of these three might be Harry Hat Man's favourite animal — a hippo, a horse or a hedgehog? (There are no wrong answers!) Your aim is to encourage word and sound recognition.

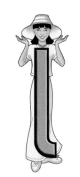
Lucy Lamp Light

● Finally, just go on enjoying the book together. Spend time talking about the pictures and what it might be like to go to Letterland. And remember always to give plenty of praise and encouragement.

To give children a real head-start with reading, there's a wealth of other Letterland products available, from audio cassettes and flashcards to activity books and ABC books. See page 32 for details.

Munching Mike

Red Robot

Quarrelsome Queen

Peter Puppy

Oscar Orange

Noisy Nick

Swinging High!

See Annie Apple, she's holding on tight.
"I don't want to fall," she says. "Not from this height!"
Her acrobat friend is swinging so high,
you'd think she could fly to the top of the sky.

Bouncy Ben Plays Ball

Bouncy Ben, that's his name.
Baseball is his favourite game.
To hit the ball a long, long way
he has to practise every day.

Clever Cat's Party Surprise

I wonder how long Clever Cat had to wait
before she could burst through the top of the cake.
She must have been curled up tightly inside,
and had to be quiet in order to hide.

She tucked in her tail so she wouldn't be seen.
It must have been hard not to eat all that cream.
Then all of a sudden the cake starts to rise,
And out of the top leaps a furry surprise!

Hurry Home, Sweet Ducklings

Dippy Duck calls for her ducklings.
It's nearly the end of the day.
"Where are my little ones hiding?
They cannot be too far away."

"Come, my sweet ducklings, come quickly.
It's time you came home to bed."
But the ducklings would rather stay up
and play hide and seek instead!

Eddy Elephant's Exercise

Eddy Elephant is big and strong.
He weighs an amazing half a ton.
Yet in spite of his size he can win any prize,
Because Eddy gets plenty of exercise!

Firefighter Fred to the Rescue

The ground is very dry – it hasn't rained for days.
The little creatures cry, "The hay is all ablaze!"
The fire begins to spread, and all the animals flee.
But here comes Firefighter Fred: "Now just leave this to me!"
Across the field he dashes, and turns his hose full on,
then out the water gushes, and soon the flames are gone.

Golden Girl's Great Win

Go-carting's fast and furious,
and racing is lots of fun.
The last lap is almost over.
and Noisy Nick's nearly won.

But just as he takes the last corner,
he skids round the bend in a spin.
And Golden Girl soon whizzes past him,
to claim an incredible win!

12

Hooray for Harry Hat Man!

Hip, Hip, Hip Hooray!
Harry Hat Man's brought some hay.
He puts it on to Hippo's bed,
but Hippo eats it all instead!

Impy Ink's Incredible Machine

Impy has built an amazing machine –
the strangest machine that ever was seen.
It's got little cog wheels and funnels and things,
seven tanks and a dial and a timer that pings.

When the lever is pulled and the pen starts to write,
the ink on the page is a wonderful sight –
with colours of yellow and orange and blue,
red, green and violet, and indigo too!

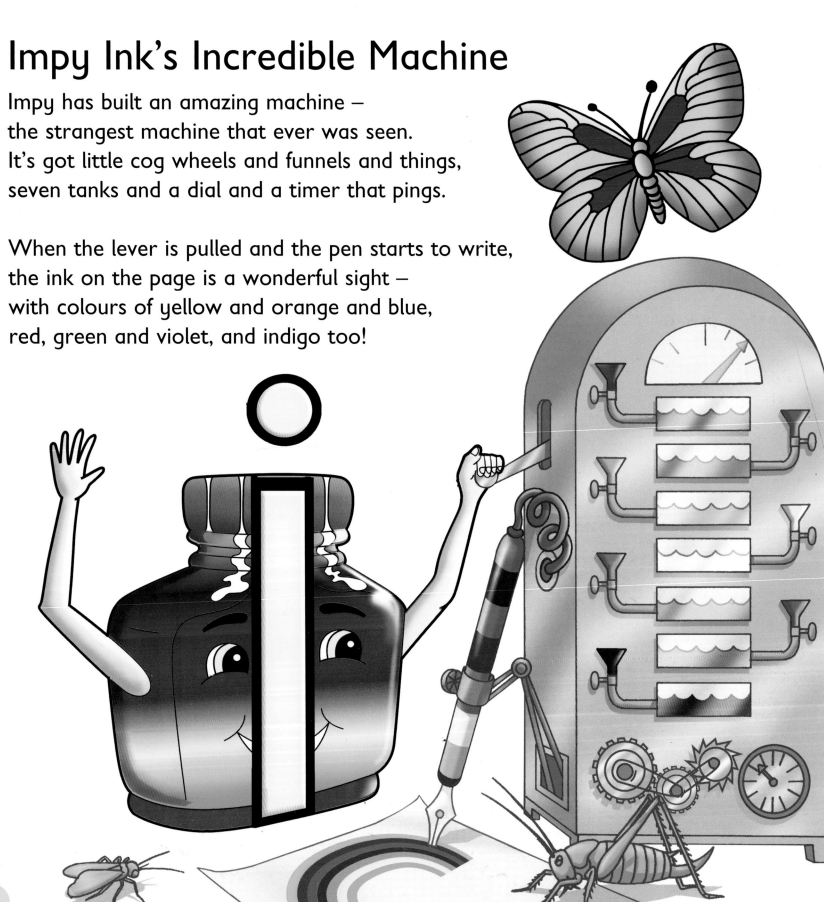

Jump Jim, Jump!

Jump Jim,
out of the way!
The jaguar's driving her jeep today.

Jump Jim,
into the sky!
A beautiful parrot is flying by.

Jump Jim,
into the air!
A friendly old toucan is sitting up there.

Watch Out, Kicking King!

Whenever the King gets a moment to spare,
he kicks lots of footballs into the air.
He puts them in rows, and kicks one by one.
He goes at great speed, and thinks it's good fun.
But the kestrel cries out, "Oh, do mind my nest.
One hit with a ball and I've nowhere to rest!"

Lucy Lights the Way

The lion cub has lost his way,
and little lamb has gone astray.
So Lucy shines her brightest light
to bring them safely home tonight.

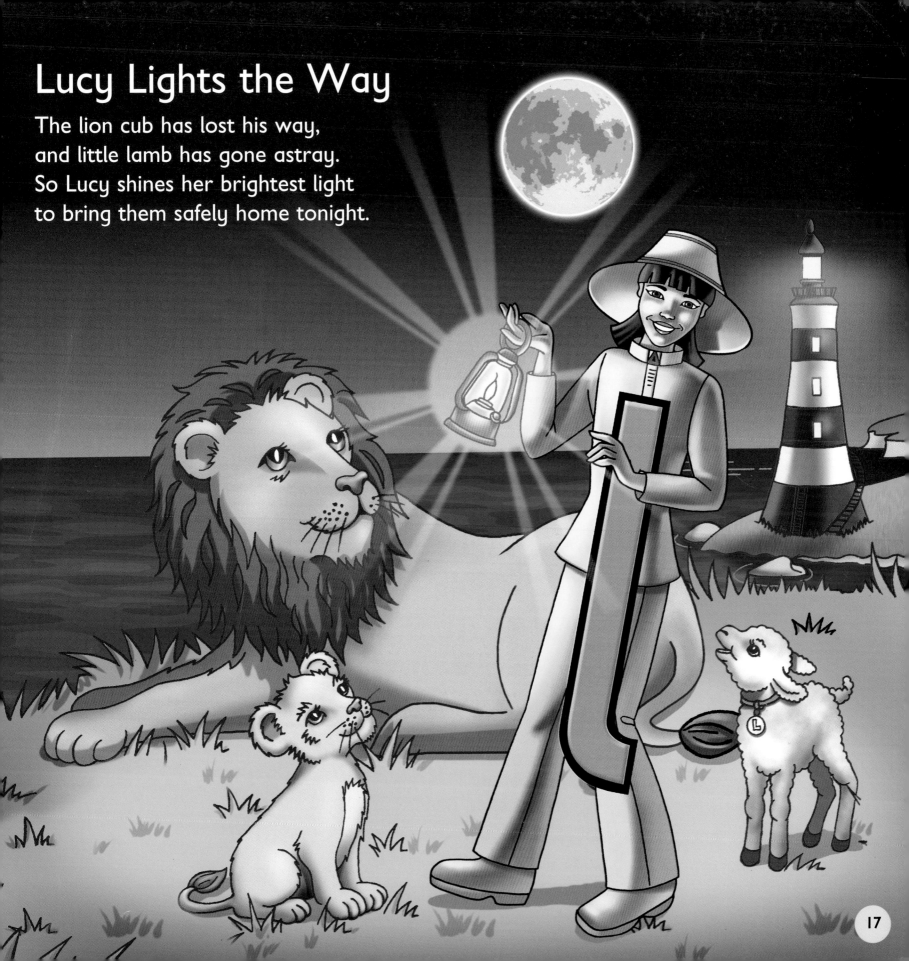

Munching Mike Under the Sea

Munching Mike just loves to be
playing with friends under the sea.
But when he goes there, he has to be quick,
or his metal will rust, and his wheels will stick.
"So goodbye crab, go hide in the sand.
I'd better go home now, back to dry land!"

Nick Gets Noisy

When Noisy Nick beats on his bongos,
the monkeys all think it's great fun.
He makes a loud noise with his banging,
so cover your ears everyone!

Oscar Orange Flies to Mars

The earth is millions of miles away,
and Oscar is flying to Mars.
But who should he see by the Milky Way?
Why, it's Zig Zag Zebra out for a play,
floating among the stars.

Peter Puppy's Parrot

When Peter plays at pirates
with a very stubborn bird,
asks Peter, "Pretty Polly,
won't you say a little word?"
But when Peter Puppy's parrot
is in no mood to talk,
the only sound she makes
is a grumpy little squawk!

Will It Rain Today?

Quarrelsome Queen
is rarely seen
without her royal umbrella.
She doesn't rely
on a sunny sky,
or believe what
the weathermen tell her!

Lost in Space

Red Robot was flying in space one day,
when some moon rock fell out of his sack.
To his dismay, it floated away:
"Tomorrow," he said, "I'll be back!"

The very next day he returned to the spot
where the dusty old boulder had been.
Though he flew all around, not a speck could be found,
and that moon rock has never been seen!

Sammy in the Sun

Just look at Sammy Snake
enjoying the fresh air,
resting in the sunshine
in his favourite chair.

But, oh, Sammy Snake,
the quiet doesn't last –
there's such a lot of screeching
with the gulls flying past!

Can You Guess?

Who's that dancing on her toes,
wearing stripey tiger clothes,
I wonder if the tortoise knows?
And, if he does, do you suppose
he'll ask the toad to have a guess?
And yes – they guess – it's Talking Tess!

Up, Up and Away

When the air is clear and the weather is dry,
Uppy Umbrella floats high in the sky.
"It's quiet up here – there isn't a sound.
And I can see mountains for miles around!"

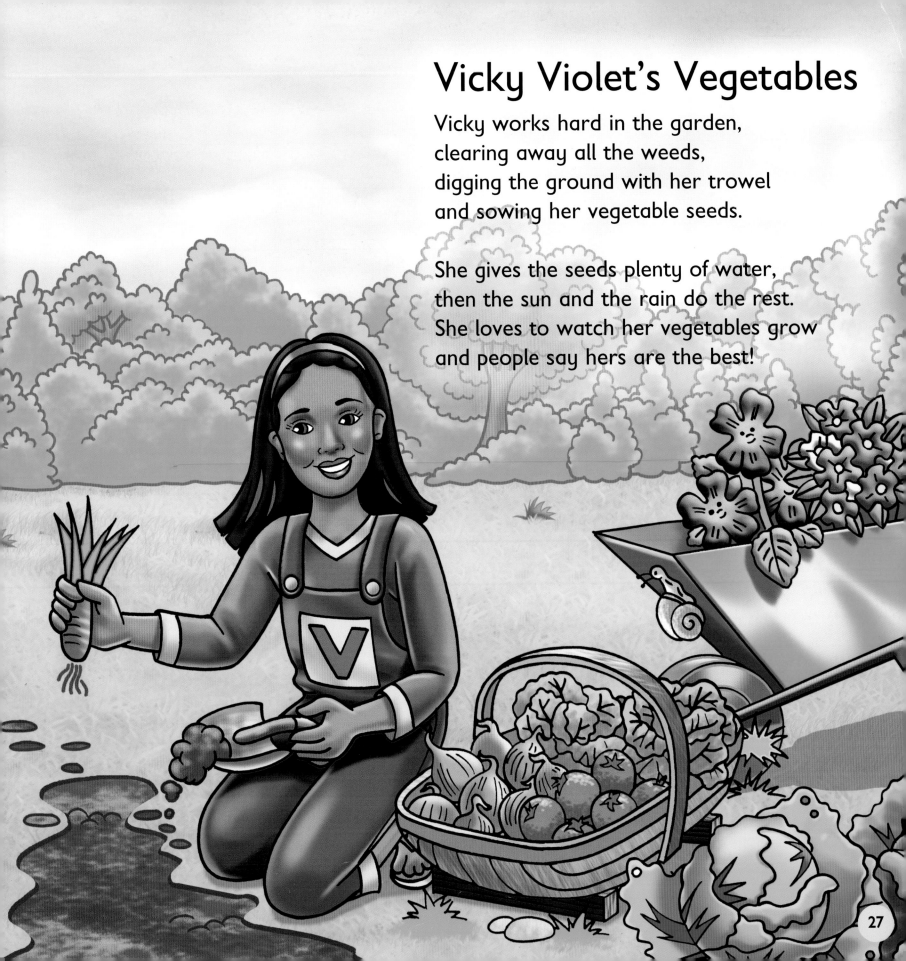

Vicky Violet's Vegetables

Vicky works hard in the garden,
clearing away all the weeds,
digging the ground with her trowel
and sowing her vegetable seeds.

She gives the seeds plenty of water,
then the sun and the rain do the rest.
She loves to watch her vegetables grow
and people say hers are the best!

A Wild and Windy Day

Walter Walrus whooshes by.
The wind is strong; the waves are high.
Baby walrus enjoys the breeze,
while Walter rides the windswept seas.

The sails upon the windmill whirl,
round and round and round they twirl.
The whales and dolphins leap and play.
It's just another windy day.

28

It's Fun to Run

Max and Maxine love to run.
The exercise is always fun.
They both keep up a steady pace,
but who is going to win the race?

The Yeti Gets a Yo-yo!

A curious yeti crept out of his cave
to see an incredible sight.
Yo-yo Man's yo-yo was spinning so fast
it was humming and flashing its light!

Said the yeti, "Oh, please, may I have one of these,
for it gets rather boring out here?"
"You certainly can," said the Yo-yo Man,
"You'll have fun for the rest of the year!"

Tickling Tigers!

Tell me, Zig Zag Zebra,
is it really true,
that you tickle tigers
lazing in the zoo?
Teasing tigers
is not wise,
once a tiger's
closed his eyes.
He may get very
cross one day,
then you'll have to
run away!

Letterland

Other Letterland titles for you to collect:

Letterland
Age 3+
Prepare for school
First **reading** activity book

Develop early reading skills

£2.99

Letterland
Age 3+
Prepare for school
First **alphabet** activity book

Meet the Letterlanders

£2.99

Letterland
Age 3+
Prepare for school
First **handwriting** activity book

Develop early handwriting skills

£2.99

Letterland
Age 4+
Prepare for school
Alphabet sounds activity book

sss...

Match letters to sounds

£2.99

Letterland
Age 4+
Prepare for school
Building words activity book

Blend letter sounds into words

£2.99

Letterland
Age 4+
Prepare for school
Reading words activity book

red

Read and spell whole words

£2.99

Letterland
ABC

Trusted by parents and teachers, loved by children

Letterland
Alphabet FRIEZE

Endorsed by teachers, loved by children

Letterland
Age 3+
First **reading** flashcards

Letterland
Age 4+
Second **reading** flashcards

Letterland
Alphabet Adventures

Letterland
Fun-to-Find Sticker Book

hen   hut
apples   map
football   shoe

Over 80 fun things to find and stick on!

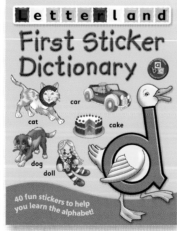

Letterland
First Sticker Dictionary

car
cat   cake
dog
doll

40 fun stickers to help you learn the alphabet!

Letterland
In the Jungle

Letterland
Under the Sea

Letterland
First Picture Word Book

plane   balloon
yacht
boat   sun bed

Trusted by parents and teachers, loved by children

Letterland
Action Songs

Full colour booklet enclosed

Sing the songs, do the actions and learn the alphabet

Letterland
Alphabet Songs

NEW EDITION

26 lively songs to help teach your child letter sounds

Letterland
Handwriting Songs

NEW EDITION

26 lively songs to help teach your child letter shapes

For more information about Letterland product, log onto our websites at **www.letterland.com** and **www.CollinsEducation.com**. Or you can e-mail us at info@letterland.com.